**Editors**
Sara Connolly
Evan D. Forbes, M.S. Ed.

**Editorial Manager**
Elizabeth Morris, Ph.D.

**Editor-in-Chief**
Sharon Coan, M.S. Ed.

**Illustrator**
Agi Palinay

**Cover Artist**
Karen Fong

**Art Director**
CJae Froshay

**Art Coordinator**
Kevin Barnes

**Imaging**
Ralph Olmedo, Jr.

**Product Manager**
Phil Garcia

**Publishers**
Rachelle Cracchiolo, M.S. Ed.
Mary Dupuy Smith, M.S. Ed.

# COM BASICS

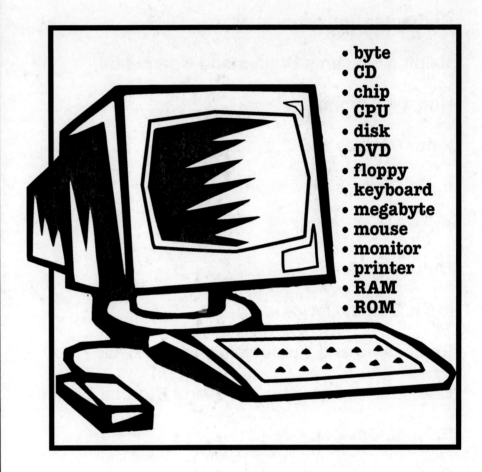

- byte
- CD
- chip
- CPU
- disk
- DVD
- floppy
- keyboard
- megabyte
- mouse
- monitor
- printer
- RAM
- ROM

**Author**

*Bill Cowan*

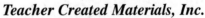

*Teacher Created Materials, Inc.*
6421 Industry Way
Westminster, CA 92683
www.teachercreated.com

**ISBN-1-55734-999-1**

*©1996 Teacher Created Materials, Inc.*
Reprinted, 2003
Made in U.S.A.

# TABLE OF CONTENTS

Introduction . . . . . . . . . . . . . . . . . . . . . . . . . . . . . . . . . . . . . . . . . . . . . . 3

Where to Begin? . . . . . . . . . . . . . . . . . . . . . . . . . . . . . . . . . . . . . . . . 4

Computer Hardware . . . . . . . . . . . . . . . . . . . . . . . . . . . . . . . . . . . . . 6

Computer Software . . . . . . . . . . . . . . . . . . . . . . . . . . . . . . . . . . . . . . 7

Helping Students Understand Computers . . . . . . . . . . . . . . . . . . . 9

How Do Computers Work? . . . . . . . . . . . . . . . . . . . . . . . . . . . . . . . 10

Input Devices . . . . . . . . . . . . . . . . . . . . . . . . . . . . . . . . . . . . . . . . . 11

Input Devices Crossword Puzzle . . . . . . . . . . . . . . . . . . . . . . . . . . 19

Processing . . . . . . . . . . . . . . . . . . . . . . . . . . . . . . . . . . . . . . . . . . . 20

Output Devices . . . . . . . . . . . . . . . . . . . . . . . . . . . . . . . . . . . . . . . 22

Input/Output Device . . . . . . . . . . . . . . . . . . . . . . . . . . . . . . . . . . . 25

Processing and Output Crossword Puzzle . . . . . . . . . . . . . . . . . . . 26

Computer Processing, Files, and Storage Devices . . . . . . . . . . . . . 27

Storage Devices . . . . . . . . . . . . . . . . . . . . . . . . . . . . . . . . . . . . . . 28

Computer Word Search . . . . . . . . . . . . . . . . . . . . . . . . . . . . . . . . . 30

Basic Ways to Use a Computer . . . . . . . . . . . . . . . . . . . . . . . . . . . 31

Making a Computer Folder . . . . . . . . . . . . . . . . . . . . . . . . . . . . . . 34

My Computer Dictionary . . . . . . . . . . . . . . . . . . . . . . . . . . . . . . . . 35

Bulletin Board Visual Aids . . . . . . . . . . . . . . . . . . . . . . . . . . . . . . . 40

Answer Key . . . . . . . . . . . . . . . . . . . . . . . . . . . . . . . . . . . . . . . . . . 48

# INTRODUCTION

The aim of *Computer Basics* is to provide students with a clear understanding of the basic principles of using a personal computer. To accomplish this, the material in *Computer Basics* is arranged in a very logical, systematic, and sequential manner. The language has been kept simple and clear so it can be understood by young readers. Wherever possible, pictures are employed to help clarify the computer terms and concepts being introduced.

*Computer Basics* contains over 75 illustrations, a number of reproducible activity sheets, and over 40 comprehension questions. A reproducible dictionary of computer terms has been included so that students have a permanent record of the computer terms that they learn in this unit. Visual aids have also been included to assist the teacher in the communication of the basic ideas of personal computing.

The topics covered in this book include the differences between hardware and software, the basic steps of computer processing, input and output devices, the Central Processing Unit (CPU) or the computer's brain, types of computer memory, storage devices, and a description of the various application programs that can be used with personal computers.

# WHERE TO BEGIN?

## Brainstorming

Beginning to teach your students about computers is not all that different from introducing them to any other topic of study. Since many of your students have previously encountered computers in their homes or at school, they will already possess some degree of computer knowledge and literacy. As with many other themes of study, a good place to start is to have your students brainstorm as many computer terms as they can. The list of computer related words found below can be used as a guide during the brainstorming session.

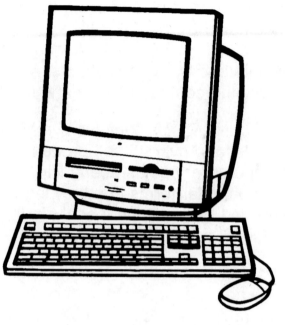

## What words come to mind when I say "computer"?

| | | |
|---|---|---|
| CD-ROM | floppy disk | network |
| computer | hardware | output |
| chip | input | printer |
| click | keyboard | program |
| CPU | modem | scanner |
| cursor | monitor | software |
| disk drive | mouse | start up |

## Assessing the Students' Existing Level of Computer Knowledge

This initial brainstorming session can be used not only as an introduction to the unit but also as a means of informally assessing your students' general level of computer literacy.

# WHERE TO BEGIN? *(cont.)*

## Creating a Unit Folder

Since there are many activity and information sheets in this unit, it will be useful to have a place to put these sheets. A unit folder is ideal. A standard piece of construction paper can be folded in half to create a 9" x 12" (22.5 cm x 30 cm) paper folder. The pictures and labels found on page 34 can be reproduced for each student. Your students can then be directed to color, cut, and paste these pictures and labels on the covers of their folders.

## Starting a Computer Dictionary

In this unit your students will be introduced to a number of concepts and terms in relation to personal computers. An excellent way of helping them retain this knowledge is to provide them with a format in which to record the information. Pages 35–39 can be reproduced for each student. The sheets can then be stapled together so as to create a personal computer dictionary where the information learned in this unit can be recorded.

Final Test Scores

## The Difference Between Hardware and Software

A good place to begin a discussion of how computers work is to help your students understand the differences between computer hardware and software. The information sheets on the next few pages should assist in this process. Since computer hardware is more concrete (can be seen and touched), it is a good place to start.

## Identifying Computer Hardware Through Matching

Once your students have talked about computer terms they can begin to identify the parts of the computer that they can touch (hardware) by simply matching pictures of these parts with their names. Have your students complete the matching activity on the next page.

# COMPUTER HARDWARE

The hardware of a computer system is all the components that you can physically touch. Some of the basic parts include the keyboard, the monitor, the case (this holds the computer's brain and other internal parts), the printer, the modem, the scanner, etc.

Can you match up the computer words found in the word box with the pictures of the parts found below?

| | | |
|---|---|---|
| monitor | printer | mouse |
| keyboard | disk drive | modem |

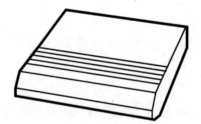

---

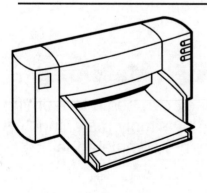

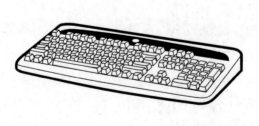

---

6

# COMPUTER SOFTWARE

The software of a computer system is the set of instructions that tell the computer what to do. This set of instructions is called a computer program. A computer program is like a cooking recipe. While recipes are often stored in cookbooks, computer programs are stored in packages called floppy disks or compact disks (CDs). While you cannot actually touch a computer program, you can hold the disk on which it is written. In order for a computer to work, it needs a program, much like a video recorder needs a videotape to play a movie.

Compact disks can hold more memory than floppy disks. A floppy disk holds about 1.44 MB of memory, while a CD holds about 650 MB of memory.

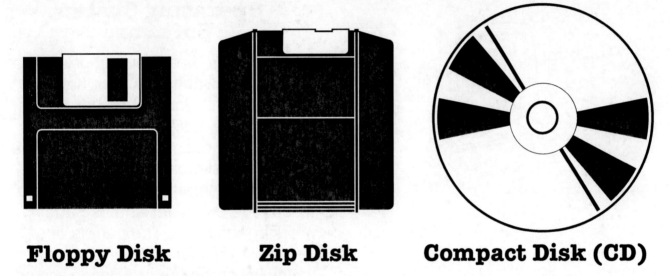

**Floppy Disk**          **Zip Disk**          **Compact Disk (CD)**

## What Have We Learned?

Read the following sentences and choose the word that goes in the blank.

1. The set of instructions that tells a computer what to do is called a_____.

    program                                    manual

2. A computer program is similar to a cooking_____.

    class                                    recipe

3. Computer programs are stored in packages called_____.

    disks                                    containers

4. A _____ can hold more memory.

    floppy disk                                    CD

# COMPUTER SOFTWARE *(cont.)*

While there are thousands of software programs for computers, there are only two main types of programs. These are operating system software programs and application software programs.

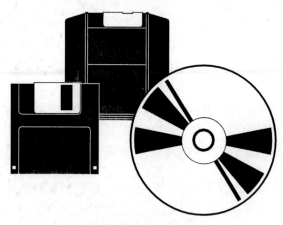

## Operating System Software

This software is a group of programs that lays down the rules for how a computer will work with other pieces of hardware, such as a modem, printer, or mouse. Much as a referee keeps a basketball game running smoothly, operating system software keeps the computer and its parts working together. The names of of the most popular operating system software programs are *Windows* and *Macintosh OS*.

## Application Software

Just as there are many recipes which allow people to make different kinds of foods, there are many kinds of application software programs that allow people to do various things on a computer. With the help of these programs, a computer can be used to make math calculations, draw pictures and graphs, sort files, and write letters. Some well-known application software programs include *Microsoft Office*, *Netscape Navigator*, and *Adobe Photoshop*.

# HELPING STUDENTS UNDERSTAND COMPUTERS

## Comparing Student Learning to Computer Processing

One way to help students understand how computers work is to compare their operation to something with which your students are familiar. Since the way that a computer processes information is similar to the way that students learn things in school, this makes for an excellent comparison. In the same way that you provide information for your students to learn and process, a person operating a computer provides information for a computer to use and process.

**Information >    Input >    Processing >    Output**

## Computer Processing

| Process Starts > | Input Devices > | Processing > | Output Devices |
|---|---|---|---|
| Computer user selects an input device to enter information into a computer. | Keyboard<br>Mouse<br>Scanner<br>Digital Camera | The computer uses its brain, called the CPU, and its electronic memory to calculate math equations, check the spelling of words, and solve problems. | Printer<br>Video Monitor<br>Sound Board<br>Audio Speakers |

## Student Learning

| Process Starts > | Input Devices > | Processing > | Output Devices |
|---|---|---|---|
| Teacher selects a method of teaching information (chart, blackboard, etc.) | Student eyes<br>Student ears<br>Student hands | Students use their brains and memory to calculate math, write, spell, and solve problems. | Students use their fingers to print out answers or mouths to speak. |

## Bulletin Board Visual Aids

Visual aids for the bulletin board have been provided on pages 40–47 to assist you in helping your students understand the sequence of processing information through the computer and the computer devices involved in this process.

# HOW DO COMPUTERS WORK?

## A Three-Step Process

There are three basic steps in the processing of information through a computer.

**Step 1: Input**—This is when information is entered into a computer. Some common input devices include the keyboard, mouse, and scanner.

**Step 2: Processing**—This is when the information is handled by a computer's brain, known as the CPU (Central Processing Unit).

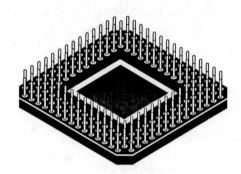

**Step 3: Output**—This is the information that comes out of a computer after it has been processed. The information comes out on output devices such as a printer or a computer screen.

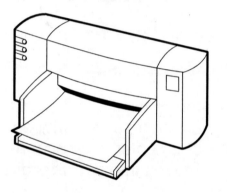

## What Have We Learned?

Read the following sentences and choose the word that goes in the blank.

1. There are_____basic steps in the working of the computer.

              5                                3

2. A keyboard is one type of input device. Another input device is a_____.

       scanner                           printer

3. The computer's brain is called a_____.

         TVA                              CPU

# INPUT DEVICES

## The Keyboard

The computer keyboard is probably the most often used input device. Its design resembles a regular typewriter. When it is used for word processing, it operates in much the same way as a typewriter. However, a computer keyboard has many additional keys that allow it to do many special things a regular typewriter cannot do.

## Computer Keys and What They Do

**Cursor Keys**

The flashing light on the computer screen is called the *cursor*. This cursor can be moved up and down or left and right on the computer screen by pressing one of the four keys that have arrows on them. These arrow keys are known as *cursor* keys.

**Letters, Numbers, and Symbol Keys**

These keys are the ones that have a letter, a number, or a symbol on them. When a letter key is pressed, that letter will appear on the computer screen. When a number key is pressed, a number will appear on the computer screen. Whenever you are using a computer to write, you will be pressing many of these keys over and over again.

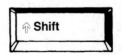

**Shift Key**

When this key is pressed at the same time as a letter key, a capital of the letter appears on the computer screen. When it is pressed at the same time as a key with a symbol and number (e.g., 4 $), the top symbol appears on the computer screen. There are two shift keys on a keyboard.

# INPUT DEVICES *(cont.)*

## Computer Keys and What They Do *(cont.)*

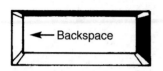

**Backspace Key** — When this key is pressed, the cursor moves back one space to the left on a computer screen. This key is very helpful when you type the wrong letter or number. By pressing this key, you can erase your mistakes.

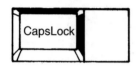

**Caps Lock Key** — When you press this key, a small light on the keyboard comes on. Whenever this light is on, any letter key you press will result in a capital of that letter appearing on the screen. Pressing the caps lock key a second time turns the light on the keyboard off.

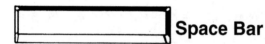

**Space Bar** — This is a long bar located at the bottom of the keyboard. Every time you press this bar, the cursor moves one space to the right on the computer screen. This space can be used before or after a letter, number, or a symbol.

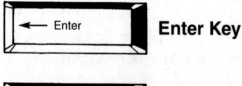

**Enter Key**

**Return Key** — When you are using a computer to write a letter or a story, pressing the enter key makes the cursor jump down to the next line. On a Macintosh computer, this is called a return key. This is a helpful key to use when you want to start a new paragraph. Pressing the enter or return key when the cursor is at the beginning of a line allows you to skip a line. The enter key is a special key that can do other things when you are not writing something on a computer.

# INPUT DEVICES (cont.)

## Computer Keys and What They Do (cont.)

### Function Keys

Most computer keyboards have between 10 and 12 function keys. These keys are usually located at the top of the keyboard and provide the computer user with a fast way to give the computer special instructions. For example, pressing the F1 key when using a Windows program will allow a computer user to easily access a help screen.

### Numeric Keypad Keys

On the right side of most keyboards there is a set of keys grouped together in a square. These keys have two functions. When the number lock key is pressed, these keys offer a quick and easy way of entering numbers into a computer. When the number lock key is not pressed, these keys control the movement of the cursor.

### Text Editing Keys

Usually located to the left of the numeric keypad are six text editing keys. These keys are designed mostly to be used in word processing programs. They allow you to move quickly around a screen when you are writing a letter or a story. They are very useful when you want to fix a spelling mistake, add a sentence to your work, or just move to another page.

# INPUT DEVICES *(cont.)*

## Finding Those Computer Keys

See if you can color the computer keys that you have learned about.

1. The backspace key is useful when you type the wrong letter. Color the backspace key **YELLOW**.

2. When the shift key is pressed at the same time as a letter, a capital letter appears on the screen. Color the shift key **BLUE**.

3. The cursor keys allow you to move the cursor around the screen. There are four cursor keys in all. Color the cursor keys **GREEN**.

4. The letter keys allow you to type words and sentences. Color the letter keys H,A,V,E and F,U,N the color **BROWN**.

5. Pressing the space bar moves the cursor one space to the right on the computer screen. Color the space bar **ORANGE**.

6. When the enter key is pressed the cursor jumps down a line. Color the enter key **RED**.

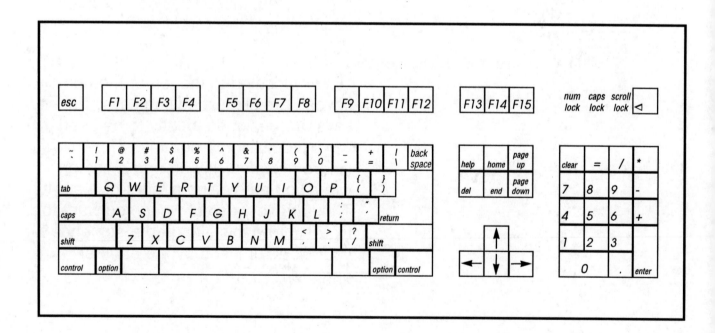

# INPUT DEVICES *(cont.)*

## The Mouse

Another kind of input device that is often used with a computer is a *mouse*. This device is shaped a little like a real mouse. In fact, the cable that connects it to the computer looks a little like the tail of a real mouse.

If you turn over the computer mouse you might see that it has a small ball inside it. This ball allows you to roll the mouse across a flat surface. When you do that and look up at the computer screen, you will see a small arrow moving across the screen. This arrow is called a *pointer*.

There is another kind of mouse that has a small ball on top of it, and to move the pointer on the screen, you roll the ball with your hand. This is called a *trackball mouse*.

One more kind of mouse is called an *optical mouse*. Instead of a ball, it has a sensor that controls where the pointer moves. The optical mouse is much lighter and can move across almost any surface without a mouse pad.

## What are the mouse and its pointer used for?

The mouse and its pointer can be used to do many things. Sometimes when you turn on your computer, there is a list of programs from which to choose. This is called a *menu*. You can use your mouse to point to one and then pick it.

Sometimes when you turn your computer screen on you see a series of pictures called *icons*. A popular program with icons is called *Windows*. You can use the mouse to choose one of these pictures. Usually, picking a picture allows you to start a program or do something within a program.

## How do you use the computer mouse?

By moving a mouse with your hand, you can make the pointer move around a computer screen until you are ready to point at an object. Usually you will find that a computer mouse has two buttons. The button on the left is the one you will most often push. Once you have the arrow pointing at the object you wish to pick, you can push the button one time, which is called *clicking*. Quickly pushing the button two times is called *double clicking* and will open whatever you are pointing at.

# INPUT DEVICES *(cont.)*

You can also move an object across the screen with your mouse. This is called *dragging*. To drag an object across the screen, point at the object, press and hold down the mouse button, and move the mouse. To drop the object at a new place on the screen, just let go of the button whenever you are ready.

## What Have We Learned About the Mouse?

1. Which kind of computer device is the mouse?_____

   input                                                    output

2. The thing that moves across the computer screen when the mouse is moved is called a_____.

   icon                                                     pointer

3. A list of computer programs shown on your computer screen is called a_____.

   menu                                                     file

4. The mouse can be used to start a program by moving the pointer to a small picture on the screen. The picture is called an_____.

   portrait                                                 icon

5. The kind of mouse that has a little ball on top of it is called a(n) _____ mouse.

   optical                                                  trackball

6. Quickly pushing the mouse button once is called_____.

   clicking                                                 tapping

7. Quickly pushing the mouse button twice is called_____.

   snapping                                                 double clicking

# INPUT DEVICES *(cont.)*

## The Digital Camera

An input device that is both easy to use and a great deal of fun is the *digital camera*. With a digital camera, you can instantly view and print any pictures that you take. You can e-mail the pictures that you take to family and friends.

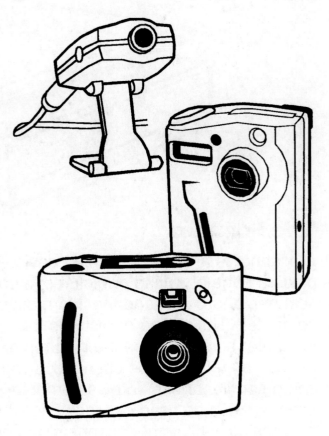

You can use a digital cameral just like you use a regular camera. You can zoom and focus on objects you are taking pictures of. Many cameras have wide-angle or panoramic capabilities.

Digital cameras do not have film. Pictures are stored in the camera's memory or on a memory card. You can preview the pictures on the camera's LCD screen. If you don't like the way a picture came out, you can just delete it.

Digital cameras often come with software to help you download the images and view them on your computer. Digital pictures can be downloaded onto Web pages, or into programs such as *Microsoft Word*, *Microsoft PowerPoint*, and *AppleWorks*.

## A Few Digital Camera Questions

1. Is the digital camera an input device or an output device?

   _____

2. What is one way that a digital camera is different from a regular camera?

   _____

3. What can you do with digital pictures?

   _____

# INPUT DEVICES *(cont.)*

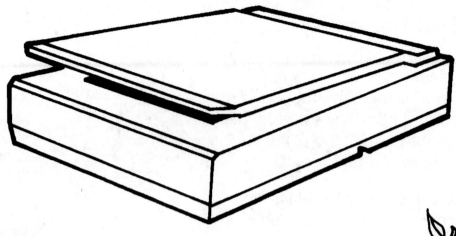

## The Scanner

A scanner is a very useful input device. You can place a page of writing or pictures in or under the scanner, and it will send the information into the computer. The writing or pictures then appear on the computer screen. Once the pictures or writing are on the screen, they can be changed, saved on a computer file, or printed by a computer printer. Some scanners can be used on black and white pictures and writing, while other scanners can be used with colored pictures.

## How Are Scanners Used?

Scanners have a number of different uses. Large amounts of information such as that found in encyclopedias, reference books, or catalogues can be scanned into a computer quickly. This can be done much faster than if someone were to type in the information. Drawings or pictures can be scanned into a computer as well. These then can be used in creating stories, reports, or newsletters.

# INPUT DEVICES CROSSWORD PUZZLE

**Word Box**

cursor

icon

keyboard

space bar

pointer

menu

clicking

digital camera

scanner

mouse

## Across

3. quickly pressing the mouse button once

4. moving the mouse moves this across the screen

6. can send a picture from a piece of paper to a computer screen

9. this device looks like a small animal

10. a long, narrow computer key

## Down

1. a small picture found on a computer screen

2. takes pictures that can be downloaded onto the computer

5. an input device that lets you type words that are displayed on your screen

7. the blinking line found on a computer screen

8. a list of programs or options

# PROCESSING

## The Central Processing Unit (CPU)

Once information is sent to a computer by one of the various input devices we have learned about, that information is then processed. Having a computer process information is similar to having a student calculate the answers to a list of math questions. Just as the student uses his/her brain to calculate the math answers, the computer uses its brain to process information. The computer's brain is called the *Central Processing Unit*, or CPU for short.

The CPU is also called a *microprocessor*. The word "micro" means small. Since the CPU is located on a small computer chip of about 1 square inch (2.5 cm²), it makes sense that it is also called a microprocessor.

## Two Types of Computer Memory

Just as a student uses his/her memory to solve different kinds of problems, a computer uses its memory to process information and solve problems.

A computer has two main types of memory. *RAM*, which stands for Random Access Memory, is the computer's temporary memory. The computer holds information in this memory and gets it when it needs it. For example, if you were writing a story on a computer, it would hold your words in its RAM until you were ready to print your story out. A second kind of computer memory is called *ROM*, which stands for Read-only Memory. This memory is permanent. The information in this memory is put there when a computer is made. A computer needs this information in its ROM memory in order for it to function.

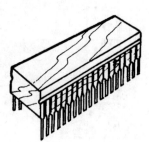

## Questions About Processing

1. A computer's brain is called the CPU.                     true     false

2. Sometimes the CPU is called a microprocessor.             true     false

3. The computer's memory called RAM is temporary memory.     true     false

4. The computer's memory called ROM is permanent memory.     true     false

# PROCESSING *(cont.)*

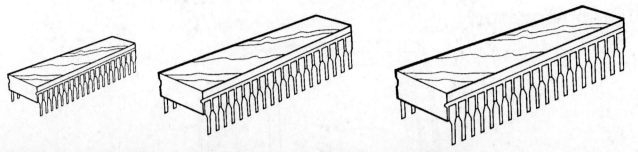

## Computer Processing and Memory Size

When a computer processes information, it uses a variety of software programs. Each of these programs requires a certain amount of electronic memory, or RAM, in order to run properly. Therefore, how well or how fast a computer can solve problems or process information depends partly on the size of its temporary memory, or RAM.

A computer's temporary memory is measured by the amount of information it can hold at one time. Each character of information (e.g., 3, f, $, &, etc.) is called a *byte*. When there are 1,024 characters together, they are called a *kilobyte*. When there are 1,048,567 characters together, they are called a *megabyte*. When there are 1,073,741,824 characters together, they are called a *gigabyte*. When the temporary memory, or RAM, of a computer is described by size, it is often said to have "so many" megabytes of memory (e.g., 4 MB, 8 MB). The table below shows the terms used to describe a computer's electronic memory.

| Term Used to Describe Memory Size | Amount of Information |
|:---:|:---:|
| Byte | One character |
| Kilobyte | 1,024 characters |
| Megabyte | 1,048,567 characters |
| Gigabyte | 1,073,741,824 characters |

**Note:** These terms are also used to describe how much information can be held by memory devices that are more permanent than RAM, such as a hard disc drive.

## Questions About Processing and Memory

1. Each character of information is called a byte.      true    false

2. When there are 1,048,567 characters of information together, they are called a kilobyte.      true    false

3. RAM is the computer's permanent memory.      true    false

# OUTPUT DEVICES

## Video Monitor

Once a computer has processed information, it needs to send the information back to the computer user (the person using the computer). A computer does this through output devices. One of the most frequently used output devices is the video monitor. The video monitor looks very similar to a television set. The types of information that can be displayed on it include words, pictures, tables, numbers, and graphs.

The size of a video monitor is measured by the distance diagonally from one corner of the screen to the opposite corner of the screen. Video monitors can range in size. Monitors have their own on/off switches and usually must be turned on and off separately from the computer.

## What Have We Learned About the Video Monitor?

1. Is the video monitor an input device or an output device?

   input                                                    output

2. Are words the only type of information that can be viewed on a video monitor?

   yes                                                      no

3. How is the size of a monitor measured?

   top to bottom                                            diagonally

# OUTPUT DEVICES *(cont.)*

## Printer

Another output device which is frequently used with a computer is the *printer*. Once a computer user has created something on a computer, such as a story or a report, he/she can display it on his/her video screen. The printer allows the computer user to print out a "typed" or "hard" copy of exactly what is on the screen.

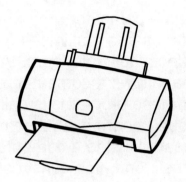

## Types of Printers

There are two main types of computer printers. One kind of printer is the laser printer. Laser printers use a laser beam to create an image that is transferred to paper. The laser printer does not use a ribbon as some older printers did. Instead, it uses a toner and a drum. The printer process with a laser printer is similar to that of the process involved in a photocopy machine.

Another kind of printer is called an ink jet printer. This type of printer shoots out small dots of ink onto the paper. The dots are very tiny and precise. Many ink jet printers can produce a variety of colors. This kind of printer is much less expensive than a laser printer. A very popular kind of ink jet printer is the bubble jet printer. The bubble jet printer uses heat to create a bubble of ink that is sprayed onto the paper.

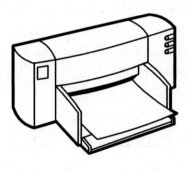

## A Few Questions About Printers

1. The computer printer prints an exact copy of what is on the video monitor.

    true                                          false

2. What kind of printer uses heat in its printing process?

    ink jet                                       bubble jet

# OUTPUT DEVICES *(cont.)*

## Sound Boards

Some computer programs such as video games and multimedia programs have sound effects built into them. A type of output device that allows a computer to produce the sounds of these programs is called a *sound board*. A sound board is an electronic circuit board, located inside a computer, that can produce music and high quality sounds.

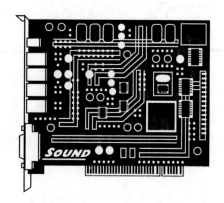

## Sound Boards and Audio Speakers

Many sound boards are able to be connected to a pair of small external audio speakers or even to a set of larger home stereo speakers. This allows a computer user to hear the very realistic sound effects of certain video games. These sounds include the sound of car engines, explosions, etc. The sound boards and audio speakers also allow a computer user to play music through his/her computer. In some instances, speech itself can be played through the speakers.

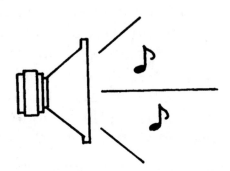

## What Have We Learned?

1. The sound board is located_____the computer.

              inside                                 outside

2. Many sound boards can be connected to external speakers.

              true                                 false

3. Music is the one kind of sound that cannot be played through external speakers.

              true                                 false

# INPUT/OUTPUT DEVICE

## The Modem

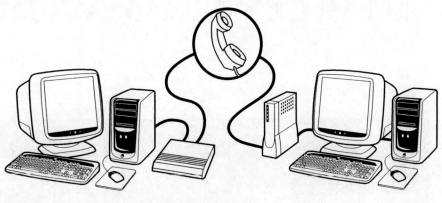

The word *modem* is a short form for modulator demodulator. It is a special communication device that is able to allow one computer to talk to another computer via telephone lines. It is similar to two friends talking to one another on the telephone. Since the modem allows the computer to both send and receive information, it is called an input/output device.

Some modems are located inside computers while others are located outside computers. Those located inside are called internal modems. Those located outside the computer are called external modems. Some modems are wireless, and send data to the computer via radio signals. In order to work, modems require special computer software called a communication program. Since a modem allows for the communication of information via telephone lines, it is also referred to as a telecommunications device. Different modems send and receive information at different speeds. Older modems connected at a speed of 28.8 or 33.6 kilobits per second. Most dial-up modems today connect at 56 kilobits per second.

Digital Subscriber Line (DSL) modems and cable modems offer high-speed Internet access without having to use your phone line to dial up every time. These kinds of modems maintain a constant connection to the Internet, so you can go online at any time while your computer is on. Cable modems can connect at a speed of 30 megabits per second, while DSL modems connect at a little less than 10 megabits per second. Cable modems use cable television lines to connect the computer to the Internet. DSL modems use telephone lines, but split the signal so that you can still make and receive phone calls while you are online.

## A Few Questions About Modems

1. Modems can both input and output information.

   true                                                    false

2. All modems are located inside the computer.

   true                                                    false

3. DSL modems do not use telephone lines.

   true                                                    false

# PROCESSING AND OUTPUT DEVICES CROSSWORD PUZZLE

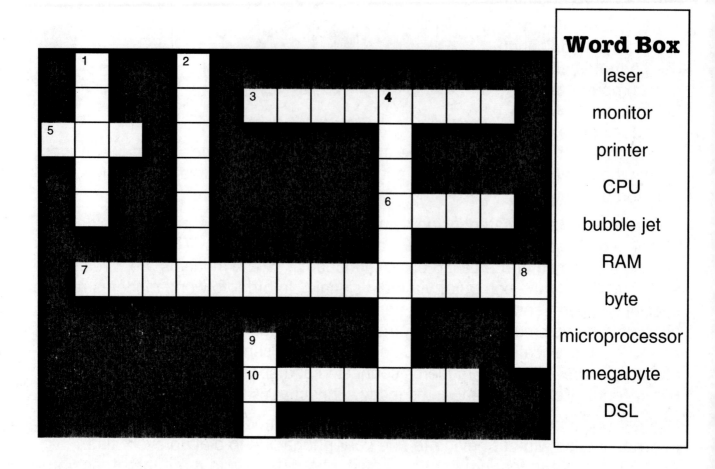

**Word Box**

laser

monitor

printer

CPU

bubble jet

RAM

byte

microprocessor

megabyte

DSL

## Across

3. This thing can hold 1,048,567 bytes of information.

5. a kind of modem that is constantly connected

6. A single character is also called a _____.

7. another name for the CPU

10. output device that gives you a hard copy of your work

## Down

1. This kind of printer uses a toner and a drum.

2. The computer screen is also called a video.

4. a kind of printer that uses heat to spray ink onto paper

8. a computer's temporary memory

9 the name of the computer's brain

# COMPUTER PROCESSING, FILES, AND STORAGE DEVICES

In learning about computer processing, we have seen that when information is being processed in a computer, it is held in a computer's temporary memory. We have also learned that this memory is called Random Access Memory (RAM). Often, information being processed in a computer needs to be held on a more permanent basis. Holding information in a more permanent way is called *saving* or *storing* information.

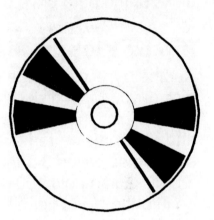

Two types of information that can be saved include data and programs. Data is any kind of information that is used in computer processing. Programs are those sets of instructions that tell a computer what to do. As mentioned earlier, programs are also called *software*. Both data and programs can be saved on a more permanent basis in what are called *files*. Data is saved on data files and programs are saved on program files.

Data or program information can be stored permanently in what are called *storage devices*. These devices are usually built right into a computer. Three of the most common storage devices built into computers today are the *hard disk drive*, the *floppy disk drive* and the *CD-ROM*.

## What Have We Learned?

1. Saving means to store information in memory more permanently.

        true                          false

2. Only data can be stored permanently in files.

        true                          false

3. Programs are also called software.

        true                          false

4. Storage devices are often built into computers.

        true                          false

# STORAGE DEVICES

## Hard Disk Drives

Most computers have a permanent storage device inside them called a *hard disk drive*. Sometimes it is also called a hard drive. This storage device contains rotating disks where data or programs are stored magnetically. The amount of information that can be saved on the hard drive is dependent on its size. The size of the hard drive, like a computer's temporary memory (RAM), is usually described in megabytes. One advantage of a hard drive is that much more information can be saved on the disks of the hard drive than on a disk of a floppy disk drive.

## Zip or Floppy Disk Drives

Another type of storage device found on a computer is called the disk drive. Most disk drives today are made for floppy disks or zip disks. This type of drive allows the computer user to save data and programs on removable storage devices. Floppy disks, sometimes called 3.5-inch disks, can store about 1.44 megabytes. Zip disks can hold 100–250 megabytes. Although the disks that go into the zip or floppy disk drives do not hold as much information as a typical hard drive, they do offer the advantage of being very portable. Information on a zip or floppy disk can be carried from place to place.

## CD-ROMs

Another storage device located in many computers is a CD-ROM drive. Like a floppy or zip disk drive, a CD-ROM is able to read data and programs that are stored on CD-ROM (Compact Disk—Read Only Memory)disks. However, while the disks that go into the floppy or zip drive can be both read and written on, most CD-ROM disks can only be read. CD-ROM disks can hold more than 783 megabytes, which means that they can hold a large number of sounds, graphics, and animations.

# STORAGE DEVICES *(cont.)*

## CD-Rs and CD-RWs

A CD-R drive is different from a CD-ROM drive.  A CD-R drive can write information such as music, data, or programs onto CD-R or CD-RW disks. You can save information on CD-R disks (or CD-Recordable disks) one time, but you can access the information over and over.  You can save information on CD-RW disks (or CD-Rewritable disks) over and over, but not all players can read CD-RW disks.

## DVDs

A DVD (Digital Versatile Disk) looks like a CD, but it can hold much more information—almost seven times more!  Many computers have DVD-ROM drives which allow you to watch DVDs on your computer.  Some computers now have DVD-R drives, which allow you to save information onto DVD-R disks.

## Understanding Storage Devices

1. In what way are data and programs stored on hard drives?

   _____

   _____

2. What is one advantage of a hard drive storage device?

   _____

   _____

3. How much data can a zip disk hold?

   _____

   _____

4. What does CD-ROM stand for?

   _____

   _____

5. How is a CD-R different from a CD-RW?

   _____

   _____

6. How much more information than a CD-ROM can a DVD contain?

   _____

# COMPUTER WORD SEARCH

There are 16 computer terms in the word box below. Find them across, down, and diagonally in the word search below.

```
U C H M O N I T O R L L X I X
P L I J O V B I T I R X Y S N
M I O L Z U H G D N I I I C C
G C P U S O S M Z P G W R A M
I K Y P T P Q E D U D M U N O
A I C U R S O R J T S V H N F
W N Q P K O Q U I P M O D E M
Z G Z E S N G H A R D W A R E
X R O M T A P R I N T E R R I
G M L U G S L A A C H Y I R Z
M N A A T Y S L V M I X C W A
H N D U L P R R X W S Z O T N
W S H S U K U P S T O M N V P
W T T Z G G O T Y W T O Y D M
D D W V G B X E W P P Q V G M
```

Cross off the computer terms as you find them in the word search.

| hardware | CPU | icon | programs |
|----------|-----|------|----------|
| cursor | scanner | input | RAM |
| output | mouse | clicking | ROM |
| DVD | monitor | printer | modem |

# BASIC WAYS TO USE A COMPUTER

We have learned about how a computer and many of its devices work. We are now ready to learn about some of the interesting and useful ways to use a personal computer. As we have seen, a computer and all its devices are called *hardware*. The programs that are used with a computer are called *software*. We have also learned that a software program is simply a set of instructions that tells a computer what to do. There are thousands of software programs that can be used with personal computers. There are business programs, game programs, and educational programs. We are going to look at four different types of programs and learn about some of the many things that the computer user can do with these programs. The programs include a word processing program, a desktop publishing program, a database program, and a spreadsheet program.

## Word Processing Programs

Whether you are writing a story, a letter, or a report on a computer, a word processing program makes your task much easier. These programs do many of the things that you would do if you were creating a story on paper. These things include erasing incorrect words, checking for spelling errors, or correcting grammar. These programs allow you to move sentences and paragraphs around. Some word processing programs do even much more than this. Some programs can number your pages for you, set your margins, change the size and style of your print, put information into tables, and create pictures.

Once you have used the program to create your written piece of work, you can use the program to save your work on a storage device such as a floppy disk or a hard drive. You can also use the program to tell the printer to print out a copy of your work.

## A Question About Word Processing Programs

In what subject is a word processing program most useful?

math          writing          science          social studies

# BASIC WAYS TO USE A COMPUTER *(cont.)*

## Desktop Publishing Programs

Desktop publishing programs are similar to word processing programs. Both types of programs involve the process of writing, and both programs allow you to do things like correct spelling mistakes, move sentences and paragraphs, and draw pictures. However, desktop publishing enables you to do many more things. You are able to combine elements from several different programs. For example, you can combine colorful pictures from one program with written material from another program and a graph from still a third program. Today, desktop publishing programs allow one person on the computer to do the same amount and quality of published work that a few years ago could only be done by a number of different people at a printing company.

A good way to understand the difference between a word processing program and a desktop publishing program is to compare them to a musical orchestra. While the word processing program is like a musician playing many notes on one instrument, the desktop publishing program is like the orchestra conductor, leading many musicians playing many notes on many different instruments.

## Understanding Desktop Publishing Programs

Which type of program can perform more jobs?

word processing program                    desktop publishing program

# BASIC WAYS TO USE A COMPUTER *(cont.)*

## Database Programs

Database programs are any programs containing large amounts of information. Some examples of these programs include encyclopedias, dictionaries, and telephone directories. One of the exciting things about the computer and its developments is that it has allowed for large amounts of information that used to be recorded in many bulky books to be rerecorded on small computer storage devices such as CDs or DVD. Whole encyclopedias are now stored on one disc. Whether you are using a computer to look up information on an exotic animal, an ancient musical instrument, or a specific type of cloud, database programs make the process fast, easy, and fun. In addition to education, database programs are very useful to businesses, medical and scientific researchers, and government agencies.

## Spreadsheet Programs

Just as word processing programs allow a computer user to write stories, letters, and reports quickly and easily, a spreadsheet program allows a user to do complicated math calculations with speed and accuracy. These programs are often used in businesses such as accounting and finance. They can also be used by families to help them budget their money, balance their checkbooks, and pay their bills. Spreadsheet programs are very useful when a computer user has a great deal of data (many numbers) to organize and analyze. These programs are also capable of creating a variety of different graphs (i.e., bar graphs, line graphs, etc.).

## A Question About These Two Programs

Which type of program deals mostly with numbers?

spreadsheet program                database program

# MAKING A COMPUTER FOLDER

## Materials Needed:

- pocket folder, file folder, or a large piece of construction paper
- scissors
- colored markers or crayons
- pencil or pen
- transparent tape or glue

## Directions:

Using the labels and pictures below, design a cover for your computer folder. If you do not want to use the pictures on this page, you may draw your own. When you are finished pasting or drawing your pictures, make sure you color them in, and then write your name in the space provided.

## My Computer Folder

## Name:_____

# MY COMPUTER DICTIONARY

**Student Name:** _____

# MY COMPUTER DICTIONARY *(cont.)*

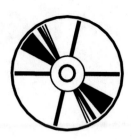

## Page 1

**Byte—** _____

_____

_____

**CD—** _____

_____

_____

**Click—** _____

_____

_____

**CPU—** _____

_____

_____

**Cursor—** _____

_____

_____

**Data—** _____

_____

_____

# MY COMPUTER DICTIONARY *(cont.)*

## Page 2

**Digital Camera—** _____

_____

_____

**DVD—** _____

_____

_____

**Floppy Disk—** _____

_____

_____

**Hardware—** _____

_____

_____

**Icon—** _____

_____

_____

**Input—** _____

_____

_____

# MY COMPUTER DICTIONARY *(cont.)*

## Page 3

**Keyboard—** _____

_____

_____

**Modem—** _____

_____

_____

**Mouse—** _____

_____

_____

**Output—** _____

_____

_____

**Pointer—** _____

_____

_____

**Printer—** _____

_____

_____

# MY COMPUTER DICTIONARY *(cont.)*

## Page 4

**Program—** _____

_____

_____

**RAM—** _____

_____

_____

**Scanner—** _____

_____

_____

**Software—** _____

_____

_____

**Video Monitor—** _____

_____

_____

**Zip Disk—** _____

_____

_____

# Input Devices

# Keyboard

# Mouse

# Digital Camera

# Scanner

# Processing

# RAM

# ROM

# Memory

# CPU

## Output

## Printer

## Video Monitor

## Sound Board

## Speakers

# BULLETIN BOARD VISUAL AIDS *(cont.)*

## Keyboard

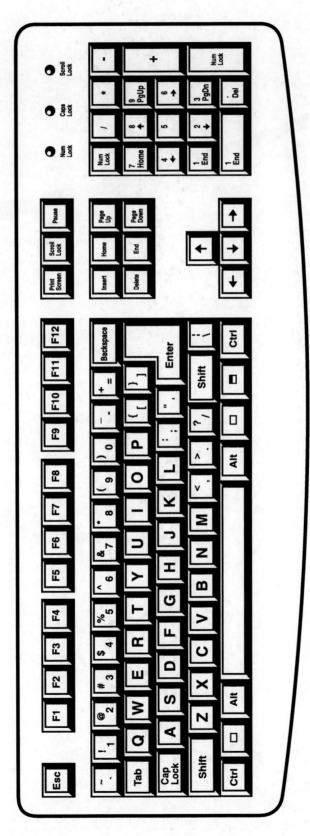

# BULLETIN BOARD
# VISUAL AIDS *(cont.)*

**Mouse**

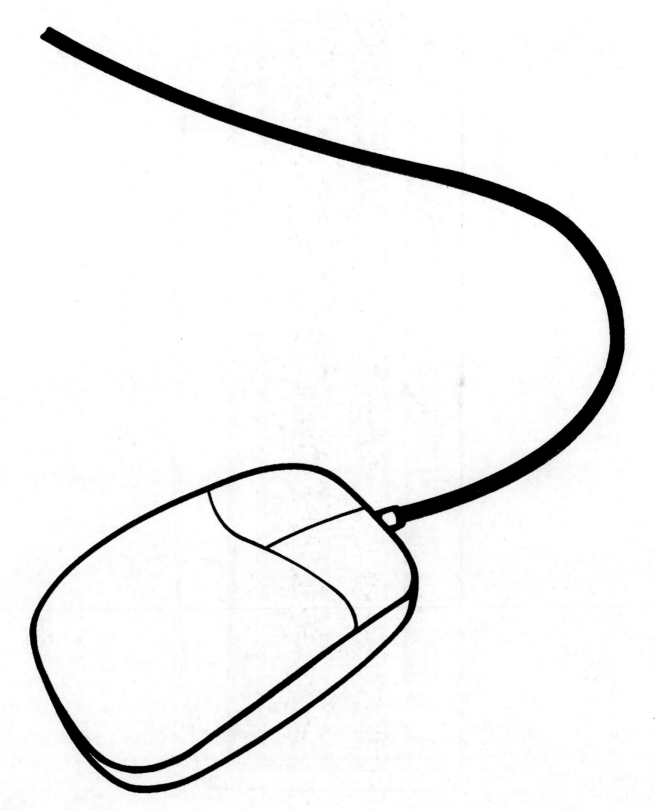

44

# BULLETIN BOARD
# VISUAL AIDS *(cont.)*

## Central Processing Unit (CPU)

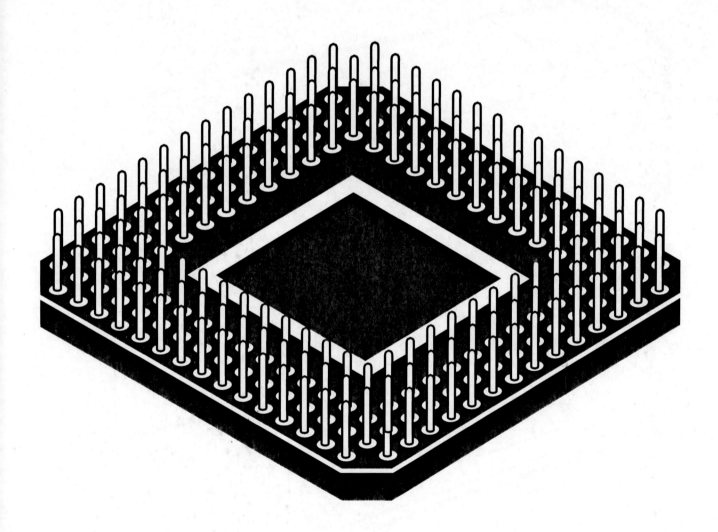

# BULLETIN BOARD
# VISUAL AIDS *(cont.)*

## Printer

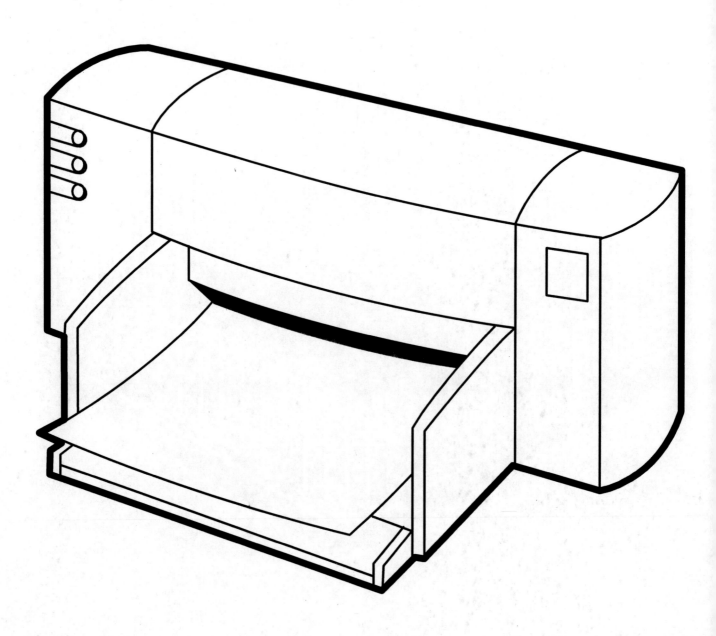

# BULLETIN BOARD
# VISUAL AIDS *(cont.)*

## Video Monitor

# ANSWER KEY

**Page 7**
1. program
2. recipe
3. diskettes
4. CD

**Page 10**
1. 3
2. scanner
3. CPU

**Page 16**
1. input
2. pointer
3. menu
4. icon
5. trackball
6. clicking
7. double clicking

**Page 17**
1. input device
2. accept answers such as does not require film, pictures can be viewed immediately, pictures can be downloaded onto the computer or into different computer programs.
3. accept answers such as print, e-mail, save, or download pictures

**Page 19**

**Page 20**
1. true
2. true
3. true
4. true

**Page 21**
1. true
2. false
3. false

**Page 22**
1. output
2. no
3. diagonally

**Page 23**
1. true
2. bubble jet

**Page 24**
1. inside
2. true
3. false

**Page 25**
1. true
2. false
3. false

**Page 26**

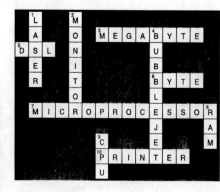

**Page 27**
1. true
2. false
3. true
4. true

**Page 29**
1. on rotating disks
2. much information can be stored
3. 100–250 Megabytes
4. compact disk—read only memory
5. CD-RW disks can be written on again and again.
6. almost seven times more information

**Page 30**

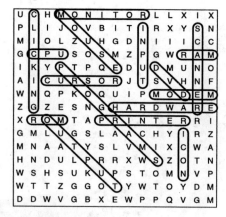

**Page 31**
writing

**Page 32**
desktop publishing program

**Page 33**
spreadsheet program